ISBN 1-55912-006-1

© Anne Geddes 1995

Published in 1995 by Cedco Publishing Company,
2955 Kerner Blvd, San Rafael, CA 94901.
First USA edition 1995
Second printing, June 1995
Third printing, September 1995
Fourth printing, September 1995
Fifth printing, October 1996
Sixth printing, February 1997

ANNE GEDDES ™

is the registered trademark
of The Especially Kids Company Limited.

Designed by Jane Seabrook
Produced by Kel Geddes
Colour separations by HQ Imaging
Typesetting by Advision
Printed through Colorcraft, Hong Kong

ANNE GEDDES

1

One pumpkin

2

Two cabbages

3

3

Three clowns

Four ducks

5

Five in a bath

6

Six flowergirls

7

Seven bunnies

Eight bees

9

Nine babies

Ten daffodils

5